Contents

LA SS Alphabetizing/Interpreting a Map 2

SS Using a Map and Map Key 4

LA Phonics–Initial Consonants 6

LA Phonics–Vowels 7

LA Phonics–Short Vowels 8

LA M Rhyming Words/Number Words 9

M Counting to Ten 10

LA Phonics–S Blends 11

M Addition and Subtraction 12

LA Positional Prepositions 13

LA SS Capitalization/Community Workers 14

LA Capitalization of Proper Nouns 15

LA M Plural Nouns/Addition Facts 16

M Addition and Subtraction Story Problems 17

LA Verbs 19

S Animal Names 20

S Predicting 21

LA S Contractions/Animal Camouflage 23

LA Days of the Week 24

M Addition and Subtraction Facts 25

LA Adjectives 26

M Geometric Shapes/Counting 27

LA Synonyms and Antonyms 28

S LA Animal Sizes/Story Structure 29

M S Bar Graph/Animal Weights 30

M Graph/Addition and Subtraction 31

M S LA Addition and Subtraction/ Animal Identification/Phonics 32

M Logic/Chart 34

M S Skip Counting by Twos/Animal Characteristics 35

SS LA Map Skills/Reading Comprehension 36

M Skip Counting by Fives 37

M Patterns 38

S Classification 39

LA Declarative and Interrogative Sentences/Punctuation 40

M LA Using a Number Code/Reading Comprehension 41

M Telling Time to the Half Hour 42

S Animal Life Cycles 43

S M Animal Characteristics/Subtraction Facts/Chart Skills 44

M Addition and Subtraction Facts/ Number Code 45

LA S Sequence of Events/Reading Comprehension/Animal Behavior 46

LA S Details/Animal Characteristics 47

M Coin Values/Addition 48

M Fractions 50

M S Fractions/Science Vocabulary 51

M Addition and Subtraction Review 52

LA Letter Form/Letter Content 53

LA Reading for Details and Cause & Effect Relationships 54

M Estimation/Counting 56

LA Writing Poetry 57

Activities to Share 58

Answers 61

We're on Our Way!

Help the Romeros and their friends get to the zoo.
Look at the names of places they will pass.
Number the words in ABC order.
Then follow the path from 1 to 8.

Try This!

Draw a map. Show how to get from your house to a
favorite place. Show the streets on which you travel.
Include the places you pass.

Which animal knows its ABCs?

The alpha-bat!

Alphabetizing/Interpreting a Map

3

What's Up at the Zoo?

Look at the zoo map and the map key.
Then follow the directions.

1. Draw a line to show a way to the Snake House.

2. Draw a ☐ to show where you can see a 🐅 .

3. Draw a △ to show where you can see a 🦆 .

Write the name of the place you would go first.

_____

4. _____

Write **yes** or **no**.

5. Can you see an  in the zoo? _____

6. Can you see a in the zoo? _____

7. Can you see a in the zoo? _____

Puzzling Names

Write the first letter of each picture.
Read the animal name.
Write the number in its circle.

_____ _____ _____ _____

- -

1. _____ _____ _____ _____

_____ _____ _____ _____ _____

- -

2. _____ _____ _____ _____

_____ _____ _____ _____ _____

- -

3. _____ _____ _____

Try This!

Make a puzzle! You need nature magazines to cut up,
scissors, glue, and heavy paper or cardboard.
1. Cut out a large picture of an animal.
2. Glue the picture on cardboard or heavy paper.
3. Cut the picture into puzzle pieces.
4. Put your puzzle back together.

6

Phonics—Initial Consonants

©1998 School Zone Publishing Company

Water World

Say **a, e, i, o**, and **u**. These are the long vowels.
Then say the words on the fish.
Color the long vowel fish **orange**.

The other words have short vowel sounds.
Color the short vowel fish **green**.

Help the squid get to her cave.
Draw a line to connect the long vowel fish.

bat

fish

fin

me

hot

boat

crab

ten

bite

Whale

huge

swim

sea

home

Honey Bear

Honey Bear is running in circles!
She is looking for words with short vowel sounds.
Start at the arrow. Write eight words you find.
Then go the other way. Say the words.

1. _____

2. _____

3. _____

4. _____

5. _____

6. _____

7. _____

8. _____

p o t a f a s t o p a t e n t u b a t r a p

Try This!

Have an adult help you make this honey of a treat.

2 apples, cored & peeled   1/2 cup walnut pieces
1/2 cup raisins   1/4 cup apple juice
1 tablespoon honey   8 Graham crackers

1. Chop the apples, walnuts, and raisins.
2. Stir in the juice and honey.
3. Spread on crackers. Eat!

A Cool Rhyme

Read the rhyme.
Then draw a line under each number word.

Penguin Pals

Five little penguin pals resting on the shore.

One took a dip, and then there were four.

Four little penguin pals walking by the sea.

One little slip, and then there were three.

Three little penguin pals with nothing to do.

One little trip, and then there were two.

Two little penguin pals looking for fun.

One little flip, and then there was one.

One little penguin all alone.

He jumped in too, and now there are none!

Write the words that rhyme with **tip**.
Say other words that rhyme with **tip**.

1. _____   2. _____

3. _____   4. _____

Quackers Pond

Look at the pond. Write how many of each.

1. _____

2. _____

3. _____

4. _____

5. _____

6. _____

7. Draw 10 🐟 in the pond.

Sneaky Snakes

Write an **s** blend to finish each picture name. Choose from these.

st   sn   sl   sk   sp   sw

1. _____ ake

2. _____ an

3. _____ ider

4. _____ unk

5. _____ ug

6. _____ arfish

Circle words with **s** blends in the puzzle.

```
x  b  s  k  u  n  k
v  s  t  o  p  s  g
s  w  a  n  g  n  s
f  t  r  y  c  o  l
t  u  f  z  j  w  u
s  p  i  d  e  r  g
y  o  s  n  a  k  e
p  q  h  s  n  a  p
```

sn sl st sp sw sk

Try This!

Play a blend game. You need six paper cups and a pen. Label each cup with one blend: sn, sl, st, sp, sw, sk. Line up the cups on a table. Toss a softball or beanbag toy at the cups. For each cup you knock over, say a word that begins with the blend.

Desert Trail

Follow the path through the desert.
Add numerals to write the **sums**.
Subtract numerals to write the **differences**.

2	+2		-1		+3

Where Are the Animals?

Where are the animals on the Desert Trail?
Finish each sentence with a word below.

over   under   in   across   on

1. The roadrunner runs _____ the _____.

2. The lizard sleeps _____ the _____.

3. The jackrabbit leaps _____ the _____.

4. The snake glides _____ the _____.

5. The owl sits _____ the _____.

Try This!

Play a game of Simon Says with family members or friends. Use the words from the oval on this page as you play.

We Work at the Zoo

Here are four people who work at Zippity Zoo.
Circle the name in each sentence.

Remember—A person's name begins with a capital letter.

Jan helps sick animals.   Bob keeps animal homes clean.

Chan teaches sea animals.   Lisa feeds hungry animals.

Write the correct name under each picture.

1. _____   2. _____

3. _____   4. _____

Try This!

To make dough names, you need 1 cup peanut butter, 1 cup honey, and 2 cups powdered milk.

1. Wash your hands.
2. Mix the ingredients in a bowl.
3. Add more milk if the dough is too sticky.

4. Form the dough into the letters of your name.
5. Eat your name!

Capitalization/Community Workers   ©1998 School Zone Publishing Company

All Aboard!

The names of special places begin with capital letters.
Zippity Zoo is a special place.
Zippity and **Zoo** begin with capital letters.
Circle the name of the special place in each sentence.

1. Parrots  live in Jungle World .

2. Ducks swim in Quackers Pond .

3. Deer run in Zebra Park .

4. Monkeys make noise on Monkey Island .

Look back at pages 4 and 5. Write the name of the
special place bears live.

Big Cat Country

A word can name one. **lion**

A word can name more than one. **lions**

Many words add **s** to name more than one.

Write a number sentence about each picture.
Add **s** to make the name of each kind of cat mean more than one.

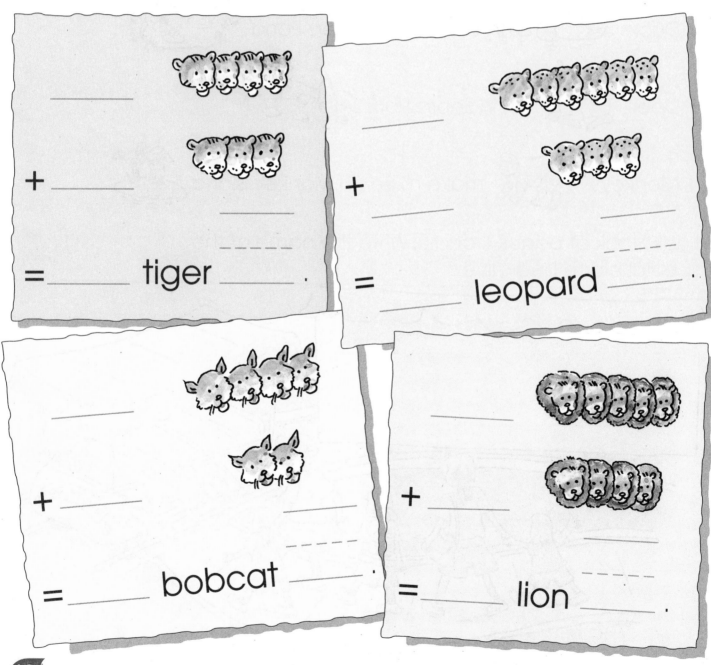

_____
+ _____
= _____ tiger _____ .

_____
+ _____
= _____ leopard _____ .

_____
+ _____
= _____ bobcat _____ .

_____
+ _____
= _____ lion _____ .

Plural Nouns/Addition Facts

Disappearing Animals

Cut out the book and put it together.
Write number sentences.
Tell the story in your own words.

8   — _____ = _____

Captain Croc's Zippity-Zoo Riverboat by

_____

_____

_____

Captain Croc  has a riverboat. Animals like to ride in his boat. Here come some now! Turn the page to begin the story.

1

6   + _____ = _____

_____ — _____ = _____

3

Try This!

Make number sentences using dominoes.
You need a set of dominoes, paper, and a pencil.
Look at the number of dots on both halves of a domino. Write a number sentence to show how many dots all together.

4 + 3 = 7

2 + 6 = 8

Addition and Subtraction Story Problems

Disappearing Animals

2 _____ + _____ = _____

7 _____ − _____ = _____

4 _____ + _____ = _____

5 _____ − _____ = _____

Try This!

1	2	3	4
5	6	7	8
9	10	11	12

Make this game board. You need a large piece of paper, chalk, and coins, buttons, or stones. Use the chalk to make the game board inside on the paper or outside on the sidewalk. Toss two coins or buttons on a paper game board or two stones on a large chalk game board. Subtract the smaller number from the larger number.

Addition and Subtraction Story Problems

Play Like the Animals

Action words tell what people and animals do.
Under each picture, write an action word from the oval.
Then draw lines to match the children with the
animals doing the same actions.

climb **dig** **slide** **jump**

1. _____

2. _____

3. _____

4. _____

Baby Talk

Some baby animals have names that are different from their parents. A baby pig is a **piglet**. What is a baby cat?

Draw a line from each baby to its parent.

calf

lamb

gosling

pup

fawn

cub

Write a baby animal name to finish each sentence.

1. **Seal** goes with _____. 2. **Tiger** goes with _____.

Let Me Out!

Some animals hatch from eggs.
Look at these eggs.
Write the name of each animal.

fish   snake
chick   robin

I sing in spring!

1. _____

I love water.

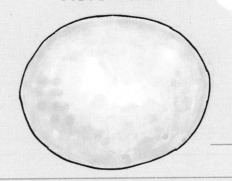

2. _____

I say sssss.

3. _____

I'm yellow.

4. _____

Hold the page up to a light or window.
Take a peek inside each egg.
Put a ✓ by the eggs you guessed correctly.

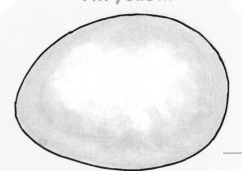

Try This!

Fill a jar with candies, cotton balls, or marbles. Ask family members to guess how many are in the jar. Write down their guesses. Take a guess yourself. Then count the number. Whose guess was closest?

Let Me Out!

Were your guesses correct?
Write the animals you got wrong.

fish   snake
chick   robin

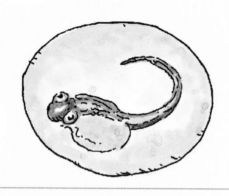

_____

- - - - - - - - - - - - - - -

_____

- - - - - - - - - - - - - - -

_____

- - - - - - - - - - - - - - -

_____

- - - - - - - - - - - - - - -

Try This!

Animals use many different things to build their nests.
You can build a nest, too. You need twigs, sticks, feathers,
string, grass, and plastic eggs.
1. Weave small sticks and twigs together to make a bowl-shaped nest.
2. Line the nest with soft things like feathers, bits of string, and grass.
3. Put the plastic eggs inside your nest.

Hiding Places

A contraction is two words put together to make one word.
A letter or letters is left out.
An apostrophe (') takes the place of the missing letter or letters.

are not ⟶ are n t ⟶ aren't

Circle the contraction in each sentence.
Then circle the animals in the jungle.

> Where's the gecko?

> Let's look for the tree frog.

> I can't find the snake.

> The toucan isn't in the tree.

Draw a line from each contraction to the words that form it.

1. can't   Where is
2. Let's   can not
3. Where's   is not
4. isn't   Let us

Contractions/Animal Camouflage

What's Happening This Week?

Read the zoo calendar.

Sunday	Monday	Tuesday	Wednesday	Thursday	Friday	Saturday
Sheep Shearing	Birthday Party for Coco the Camel	Storytime Safari	The Zoo Is for You Day!	Jungle Day Walk	Desert Trail Hike	Spring Egg Hunt

Write the day when these things happen.

1. _____

2. _____

3. _____

4. _____

Try This!

Make a days of the week journal. You need seven sheets of paper.
1. Write the name of a day on each page. Start with Sunday.
2. Each day, draw a picture or write about something you did.
3. Make a cover for your journal.

Sheep Shearing Today!

Write a number sentence about each picture.

_____ + _____ = _____

1.

_____ − _____ = _____

2.

_____ + _____ = _____

3.

_____ − _____ = _____

4.

_____ + _____ = _____

5.

_____ − _____ = _____

6.

Addition and Subtraction Facts

Describe It!

Describing words tell about naming words.
   The **huge** lion roared.
Which word tells about, or **describes**, the lion?
Some describing words tell how animals look or feel.

Write words that tell about the animals.

long   tall   tiny   wet   **sleepy**   huge

1. _____

2. _____

3. _____

4. _____

5. _____

6. _____

What a Shape!

Draw an alligator.
Follow these steps.

1.

2. Add.

3. Add.

4. Add.

Draw a tiger.
Follow these steps.

1.

2. Add.

3. Add.

4. Add.

1. How many △s
   in step 4?

_____

2. How many ○s
   in step 4?

_____

Try This!

Think of an animal. Make up a riddle about it. Tell how the animal
looks, feels, and sounds.
Example: I'm thinking of a small bird with a red head. It makes
a rat-tat-tat noise. What is it? (A woodpecker)

Monkey Business

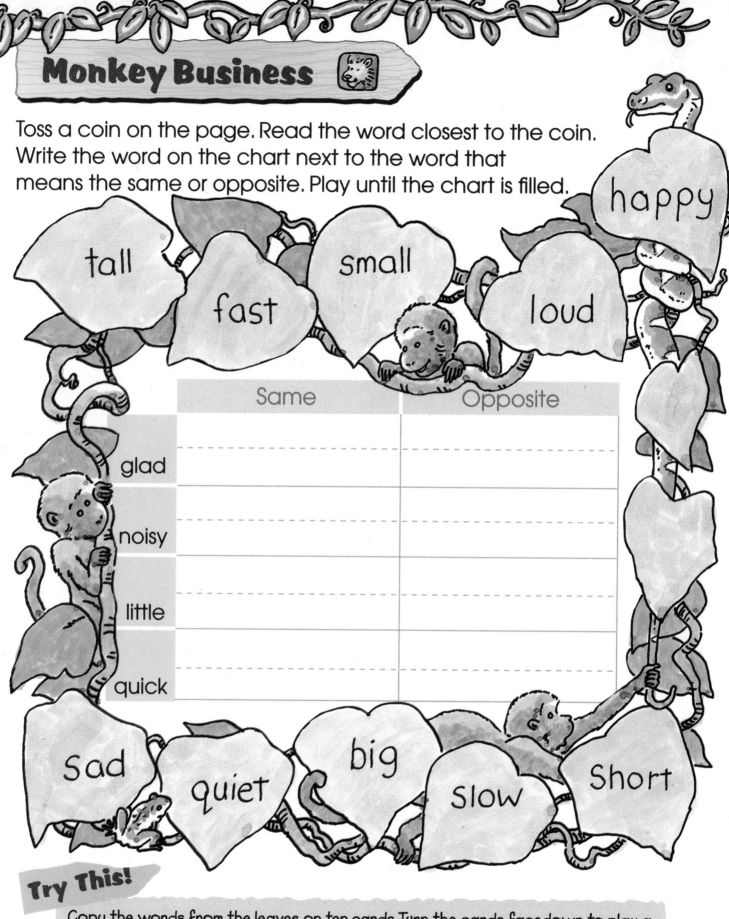

Toss a coin on the page. Read the word closest to the coin. Write the word on the chart next to the word that means the same or opposite. Play until the chart is filled.

tall

fast

small

loud

happy

	Same	Opposite
glad		
noisy		
little		
quick		

sad

quiet

big

slow

short

Try This!

Copy the words from the leaves on ten cards. Turn the cards facedown to play a game. Turn over two cards at a time. If the words mean the opposite, set the pair aside. If not, turn them facedown again. Play until you have matched all the words.

Synonyms and Antonyms

Big Meets Little

Read the names of the big and little animals.
Add two more names to the chart.

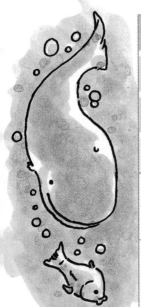

Big Animals	Little Animals
hippo	chipmunk
elephant	butterfly
giraffe	chick

Plan a story about two animals. Write your ideas.

Which big and little animals meet?

_____

_____

Where do they meet?

_____

_____

What is their problem?

_____

_____

How is the problem solved?

_____

_____

Animal Sizes/Story Structure

Little Weight Watchers

Read the scales.

Color in the boxes to show how many pounds each animal weighs.

	1	2	3	4	5	6	7	8	9	10
tiger cub										
baby porcupine										
fox										
snowy owl										
fawn										
opossum										
weight in pounds	1	2	3	4	5	6	7	8	9	10

Bar Graph/Animal Weights

You need 15 coins or buttons. Read the chart to find out how many to put in or take out of the pool.
Then count how many are left. Write the numerals in the chart.

Put In	Take Out	How Many Are Left?	Put In	Put In	How Many in All?
9	2		9	6	
10	4		2	8	
12	7		6	5	
8	6		7	7	
15	8		8	6	

Try This!

Use the coins or buttons to write as many different math equations that equal 15 as you can. Then write equations with three numerals that equal 15. Example: 6 + 3 + 6 = 15

Graph/Addition and Subtraction

Zoomobile Tour Game

You need a coin to toss, two buttons for markers, and a sheet of paper and pencil to keep score.

1. Put your button on Start.
2. Toss the coin. If it's heads, move one space.
   If it's tails, move two spaces.
3. Follow the directions on the square on which you land.
   Make a mark on the score sheet for each right answer.
4. The game is over when you reach Finish.
   The most points wins.

Start

Stuck in the mud.
Lose 2 points.

Name it.
4 points

Subtract it.
11 − 6 = ___
2 points

Name it.
2 points

Name it.
4 points

Name it.
3 points

Finish the word.
___ OX
1 point

Name it.
2 points

Name it.
4 points

What's missing?
2, 4, 6, ___, 10.
3 points

Run out of ga__
Lose 3 points

Add it.
8 + 4 = ___
1 point

You're lost.
?, ? ? ?
Lose 1 point.

Addition and Subtraction/Animal Identification/Phonics

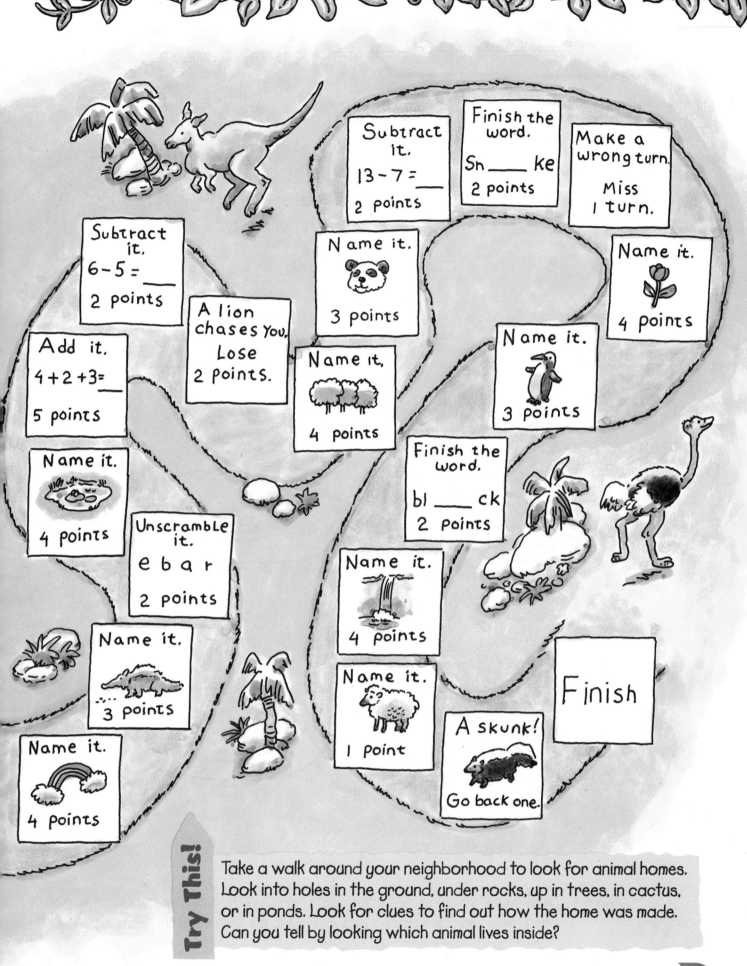

Subtract it.

13 − 7 = ____

2 points

Finish the word.

Sn ____ ke

2 points

Make a wrong turn.

Miss 1 turn.

Subtract it.

6 − 5 = ____

2 points

Name it.

3 points

Name it.

4 points

A lion chases you. Lose 2 points.

Name it.

4 points

Name it.

3 points

Add it.

4 + 2 + 3 = ____

5 points

Name it.

4 points

Finish the word.

bl ____ ck

2 points

Unscramble it.

e b a r

2 points

Name it.

4 points

Name it.

3 points

Name it.

1 point

A skunk!

Go back one.

Finish

Name it.

4 points

©1998 School Zone Publishing Company

Try This!

Take a walk around your neighborhood to look for animal homes. Look into holes in the ground, under rocks, up in trees, in cactus, or in ponds. Look for clues to find out how the home was made. Can you tell by looking which animal lives inside?

Addition and Subtraction/Animal Identification/Phonics

Critter's Cafe

Read the clues. Mark the chart with ✓s.
The first one is done for you.

1. Everyone had fruit.
2. Dad and Ben had a taco.
3. Mom had a salad.
4. Anna had a turkey sandwich.
5. Mom, Ben, and Anna had juice.
6. Dad had milk.

	milk	juice	fruit	salad	taco	sandwich
Dad			✓			
Ben			✓			
Mom			✓			
Anna			✓			

Write a person's name under each meal.

1. _____

2. _____

3. _____

4. _____

Start at 2. Connect the dots counting by twos from 2 to 40.

• 8   • 10

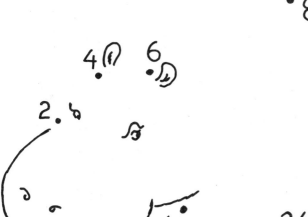

4 • 6
2 •
• 12
40   • 34   • 28   • 26   • 20   • 14

38   36   • 32   • 30   • 16
          2 4   2 2   1 8

Read more clues about this animal.
Write the words from the circle in the sentences.

hippo
grass
fat water

_____

1. This animal is very _____ .

2. It spends the day in _____ and eats at night.

3. It can eat 88 pounds of _____ each night.

4. This animal is a _____ .

Skip Counting by Twos/Animal Characteristics

35

Who Is Lost?

Dad went to buy popcorn. Now he is lost.
Circle the right answers to help him find the family.

1. Where should Dad walk first?

   to the office   to the water fountain   to the zoo entrance

2. Next, Dad should walk to the ___.

   flag   trash can   pond

3. Dad will see the family on the bench if he walks by the ___.

   office   pond   parrot

4. Write **1, 2, 3** to show the right order.

   _____ flag   _____ fountain   _____ parrot

5. Draw a red line on the path Dad should take.

Ape Escape

Help the ape get to the banana tree.
Count by fives from **5** to **50**.
Color the squares with these numbers to show the path.

5	10	6	22	13	8
11	15	7	18	31	14
17	20	25	32	47	71
36	22	30	35	40	48
51	56	43	33	45	50

Try This!

Try counting backwards from 50 to 5.
Then count by twos from 30 to 2. Count
by tens from 100 to 10. How fast can
you count?

Skip Counting by Fives

Look at each row.
Draw the missing picture to fit the pattern.

1.

2.

3.

4. Help the tiger get to her cubs. Find the pattern.
   Color the shapes to finish the path.

Try This!

Collect leaves and flower petals.
Glue them on paper to form
different patterns.

Get Out of Here!

Look at each group of animals.
Circle the one that does not belong.
Then draw an animal that belongs.

A telling sentence ends with a period. (.)
An asking sentence ends with a question mark. (**?**)

Read the sign. Add a (.) or a (**?**) in the ◯ at the end of each sentence.

Forest Theater

1. The theater is open from 9:00 to 5:00 ◯

2. Have you ever seen an opossum ◯

3. Do you know what a deer eats ◯

4. Come see the show to find out ◯

5. You will meet many forest friends ◯

Declarative and Interrogative Sentences/Punctuation

The Big Screen

Write the letters under the numbers.
The first letter is done for you. Then read each animal name.
Draw a line to match the name to the picture.

1	2	3	4	5	6	7	8	9	10	11	12	13	14	15	16
a	b	c	d	e	i	k	l	m	n	o	p	q	r	s	u

The Stars of the Show

1.
11	12	11	15	15	16	9
o						

2.
4	5	5	14

3.
15	7	16	10	7

4.
15	13	16	6	14	14	5	8

Try This!

Finish this riddle about one of the stars of the show. Write your own words. Ask someone to guess your riddle.

This animal lives in the forest.
Its color is _____.
It has _____.
What is it?_____.

Using a Number Code/Reading Comprehension

When does each animal get up in the morning?
Write the time.

: _____   : _____   : _____

: _____   : _____   : _____

**What do you say to a
clock at noon?**

Hands up!

Froggy Grows Up

Look at the pictures.

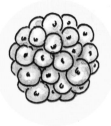

A

B

C

D

E

Read the sentences.
Write **A**, **B**, **C**, **D**, and **E** to show how froggy grows up.

1. _____ Froggy is a tiny tadpole.

2. _____ Froggy is a big frog.

3. _____ Froggy is an egg.

4. _____ Froggy grows four legs.

5. _____ Froggy grows two legs.

Animal Poll

The zookeeper is counting the animals with hooves.
She needs more animals for the zoo.
Fill in the chart to show how many more she needs.

Kinds of Animals		Animals We Want	Animals We Have	How Many More Do We Need?
camel		8	4	
deer		15	9	
giraffe		10	7	
hippo		12	8	
pig		14	7	
sheep		18	9	
buffalo		9	5	
moose		13	6	

Try This!

Have you ever seen an old nickel with a picture of a buffalo on it?
You can design your own nickel.
1. Cut a large circle from paper or use a white paper plate.
2. Choose an animal for your coin.
3. Draw what your coin will look like.

Animal Characteristics/Subtraction Facts/Chart Skills

Who Is Hiding?

One animal with hooves is very shy.
He is hiding behind these numbers.
Find the sums and differences of the numbers in each row.
Then use the code to find out the animal's name.

7	8	9	10	11	12	13	14	15
r	e	s	m	t	o	f	s	v

5	12	8	5	10
+8	-6	+2	+7	-3
-7	+3	-5	-6	+7
+4	+3	+7	+8	-6

Look at the last number in each row. Write the letter from
the code box to spell the animal's name.

____ ____ ____ ____ ____

Addition and Subtraction Facts/Number Code

Read the story.

Last night we saw some **tracks**. The tracks came from the

forest . They went by the tree . Then they went

down to the pond . We followed the tracks to our

house . What is all that noise? A hungry visitor is eating dinner!

Look at the yard. Follow the tracks.
Number the places from 1 to 4.

Be a Detective

Look at the story on page 46.
Answer the questions.

1. A fox has four toes on each paw.
   Is the visitor a fox?   Yes   No

2. A deer has hooves.
   Is it a deer?   Yes   No

3. A raccoon has five toes on each paw.
   Is it a raccoon?   Yes   No

4. **What** did you see?

   _____

   _____

5. **Where** did they come from?

   _____

   _____

6. **When** did this happen?

   _____

   _____

Look for tracks in your yard.
1. Go outside. Spread some sand on the ground.
2. Place bird seed, nuts, bread, and fruit slices in the center.
3. Stay away for a day. Then check for animal tracks.
4. What do you see? Three toes might mean a bird was there.
   Four front toes and five back toes might mean a squirrel or chipmunk.

Details/Animal Characteristics

Making Cents

Count the money. Write the amounts on the lines.
Is there enough money to buy the item?
Circle **Yes** or **No**. The first one is done for you.

1. <u>25¢</u> <u>10¢</u> <u>10¢</u> <u>5¢</u>   Yes ⓃⓄ

2. _____ _____ _____ _____   Yes   No

3. _____ _____ _____ _____   Yes   No

4. _____ _____ _____ _____   Yes   No

Try This!

Play Yard Sale with some friends. Use self-stick notes to label prices on things around the house. Buy and sell the things you labelled using coins or play money.

Write the price of each item. Then add and write the total.

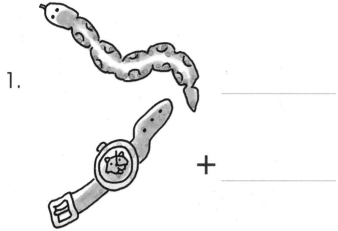

1. _____

\+ _____

How much for both? _____

2. _____

\+ _____

How much for both? _____

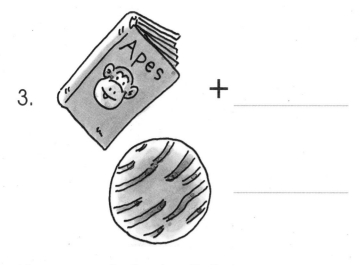

3. _____

\+ _____

How much for both? _____

4. _____

\+ _____

How much for both? _____

Coin Values/Addition

Parts of a Whole

A fraction is a part of a whole.

$\dfrac{1}{4}$ → part shaded
→ parts in all

Color the shapes to show the fractions.

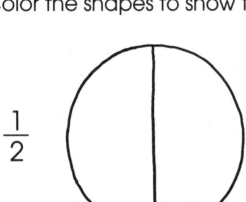

$\dfrac{1}{2}$

$\dfrac{1}{4}$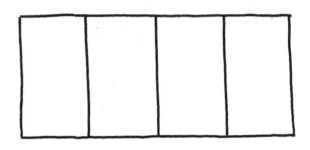

$\dfrac{1}{3}$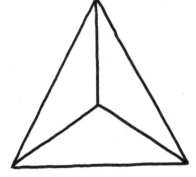

$\dfrac{2}{2}$

$\dfrac{3}{4}$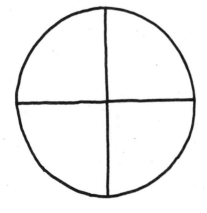

$\dfrac{2}{3}$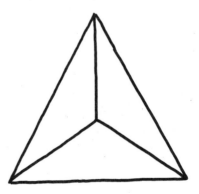

Let's Eat!

What do zoo animals eat? Draw a line from each word to the food. Color foods in each group to show the fraction.

apples   carrots   bananas   oranges   hay   lettuce

1. $\dfrac{2}{4}$

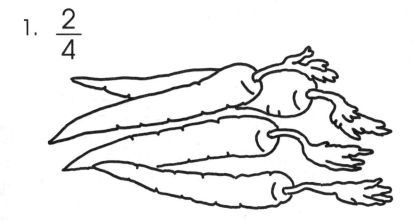

2. $\dfrac{2}{5}$

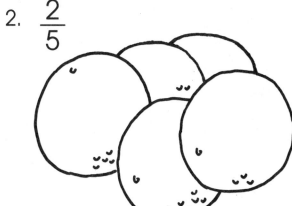

3. $\dfrac{1}{3}$

4. $\dfrac{1}{4}$

5. $\dfrac{2}{3}$

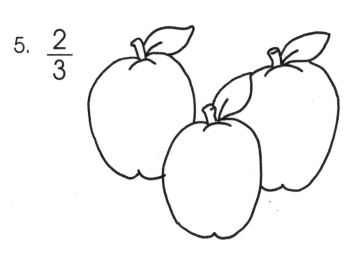

6. $\dfrac{1}{2}$

Fractions/Science Vocabulary

Butterfly Garden

Take the family through the butterfly garden.
Answer each problem in the space that
follows it. Then circle the hidden butterflies.

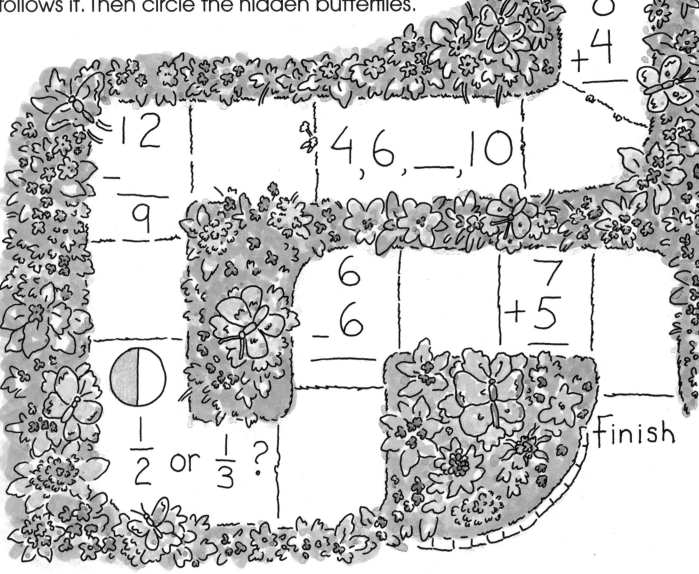

Start

8
$+4$

12
-9

$4, 6, \_\_, 10$

6
-6

7
$+5$

Finish

$\dfrac{1}{2}$ or $\dfrac{1}{3}$?

How many butterflies did you find? _____

Try This!

The right half of a butterfly is the same as
the left half. You need paper, scissors, and
crayons. Fold a sheet of paper in half. Draw
half of a butterfly. Cut out the shape. Then
unfold it. Color both halves the same way.

Addition and Subtraction Review

Animal Pen Pal

Pretend you are an animal at a zoo.
Write a letter to the visitors.
Remember to sign your name as the animal.

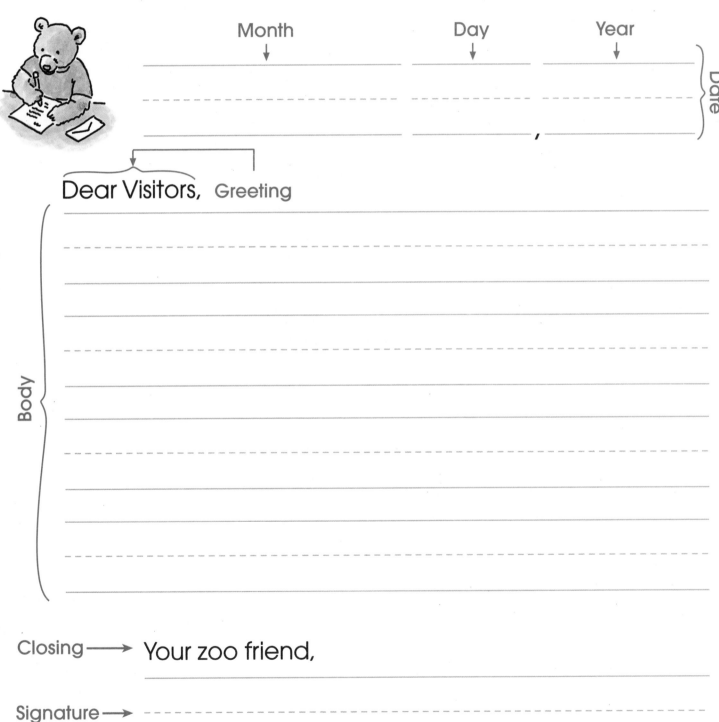

Month   Day   Year

Date

Dear Visitors,   Greeting

Body

Closing ⟶ Your zoo friend,

Signature ⟶

Letter Form/Letter Content

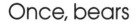

A bear's tail is short and stubby.
One Native American tale explains why.

Once, bears had **long, furry tails**. Then something

happened. Bear  was hungry for crayfish  .

But the pond was frozen. So Bear  asked

Fox  for help. Tricky Fox  told Bear

to make a hole in the ice. He told Bear to hang his long

tail through the hole. When a crayfish  pinched it, he

could pull the crayfish  up. Bear  felt a

pinch. But it it was not a crayfish  . His tail was frozen into

the pond . Bear  pulled so hard that his tail

broke off. Bears have had **short tails** ever since.

Try This!

Write your own tale. Think of an animal and what
is special about it. Tell how it got to be that way.
Draw pictures to go with your story.

How did
I get my
spots?

Reading for Details and Cause & Effect Relationships

1. What kind of tail did bears once have?

_____

- -

_____

2. What kind of tails do bears have now?

_____

- -

_____

3. Why did bears' tails change?

_____

- -

_____

_____

_____

Compare the Bears!

Black Bears: 4–5 feet long; 150–400 pounds
Grizzly Bears: 6–7 1/2 feet long; 300–900 pounds
Polar Bears: 6–8 feet long, up to 1,500 pounds
Coastal Brown Bears: 6–8 1/2 feet long; up to 1,600 pounds

Grizzly Bear

Brown Bear

Black Bear

Polar Bear

Reading for Details and Cause & Effect Relationships

Animal Count

In this picture are some of the animals
you met in this book.
Guess how many there are.

Now count the animals.
Watch out!
Some animals are hiding.
How close was your guess?

Be a Poet

There are many reasons people like zoos.
Write some of your reasons here to finish this poem.

Zoos

I like zoos.
I'll tell you why.
Because,

_____

- -

_____

Because,

_____

- -

_____

Because,

_____

- -

_____

Because! That's why!

I like zoos.

Try This!

Make an animal puppet to help you say your poem.
You need a paper bag, construction paper, scissors,
glue, crayons, and markers. Draw a face on the flap
at the bottom of the bag.
1. Cut out and add ears.
2. Add a mouth and feet, paws, or wings.
3. Put your hand inside the bag. Move the flap up and
   down to make your puppet talk.

Activities to Share: Language Arts

Here is a list of excellent animal books to look for in your local library or bookstore.
The list includes fiction and nonfiction.

- *Crocodile Smile* by Sara Weeks, illustrated by Lois Ehlert. HarperCollins, 1994. Bright picture collages enhance this book of animal songs and poems. The book comes with a cassette tape.

- *From Head to Toe* by Eric Carle. HarperCollins, 1997. A variety of familiar animals invites the reader to copy their antics as they wiggle, stomp, thump, and bend across the pages of this book.

- *The Great Kapok Tree: A Tale of the Amazon Rain Forest* by Lynne Cherry. Gulliver Books, Harcourt, 1990. The great kapok tree is in danger of being cut down. What will happen to all the forest creatures if this occurs?

- *A Hippopotamusn't and Other Animal Poems* by J. Patrick Lewis. Dial Books, 1990. This is a collection of funny verse about all kinds of animals. The humorous illustrations add to the fun.

- *How the Guinea Fowl Got Her Spots: An African Tale* retold and illustrated by Barbara Knutson. Carolrhoda, 1990. When Guinea Fowl helps her friend escape from a lion, she is rewarded with a disguise that will camouflage her.

- *How the Ostrich Got Its Long Neck: A Tale from the Akamba of Kenya* retold by Verna Aardema. Scholastic, 1995. At one time Ostrich had a short neck. That changed after an encounter with a crocodile.

- *In the Small, Small Pond* by Denise Fleming. Henry Holt, 1993. Spring has sprung, and a bright green frog leaps out of the grass and into the pond where a host of other animals make their homes. The reader follows tadpoles, minnows, turtles, dragonflies, and ducks through spring, summer, and autumn. When winter arrives, the frog burrows deep into the pond to wait for spring's return.

- *Little Elephant* by Miela Ford with photographs by Tana Hoban. Greenwillow Books, 1994. Captioned photographs depict a young elephant's adventures playing in the water before returning to the safety of its mother.

- *Penguin Pete and Little Tim* by Marcus Pfister. North-South Books, 1994. Penguin Pete is a proud father who cannot wait to show his son the wonders of their chilly world.

- *Splash, Splash* by Jeff Sheppard. MacMillan, 1994. When a group of animals unexpectedly goes for a swim, each reaction is very different. The many animal sound words make this a great read–aloud.

- *Time to Sleep* by Denise Fleming. Henry Holt, 1997. The chill in the air tells Bear that it's time for her winter-long nap. She must tell Snail, who tells Skunk, who tells Turtle. Each puts off going to sleep in order to see, smell, hear, and taste the signs of the season.

V for Vanishing: An Alphabet of Endangered Animals by Patricia Mullins. HarperCollins, 1994. Beautiful collages depict many animals that are in danger of extinction.

Here are two videos about animals.

The Animal Show Starring Stinky and Jake. Polygram Home Video. Muppets Jake and Stinky host a talk show with wild animal guests.

Really Wild Animals: Swingin' Safari. National Geographic Kids. A globe named Spin is the host on a journey to Africa. You will see how zebras, elephants, lions, and other animals grow, play, and hunt for food and learn about the climatic conditions of Africa. Others in the series: *Totally Tropical Rain Forest* and *Wonders Down Under*.

Social Studies

There are many things your family can do to help preserve the environment and help save endangered animals. Here are some suggestions.

In Your Home

Recycle everything you can: newspapers, glass, cans, aluminum, motor oil, scrap metal.
Save kitchen scraps for a compost pile.
Use phosphate-free dish and laundry soaps.
Avoid using pesticides.
Use cold water in the washer whenever possible.
Use cloth napkins and washable rags.
Reuse brown paper and plastic bags.
Use plastic storage food containers rather than foil or plastic wrap.
Turn down the heat one degree for each hour you are away from home or asleep.
Turn off lights and the television when you are not in the room.
Feed the birds; make birdhouses and bird baths.
Compost leaves and yard debris.

When Shopping

Don't buy foods in styrofoam or plastic containers if there is an alternative.
Avoid disposable items. If you must buy disposables, buy paper rather than plastics.
Put parcels in one large sack rather than many small bags.
Buy in bulk and buy locally grown products.

Science

Some experts claim that there has been a 50% reduction in the population of song-birds over the past century. Do some simple projects with your child to house and feed some feathered friends. The world's easiest birdhouse to make uses a 6" to 8" green-and-orange gourd. Drill or whittle an opening for the bird. Scrape out the seeds. Drill or whittle a 1/2" drain hole at the bottom and a 1/4" hole through the top to insert a line for hanging. This house will last for one season.

To feed the birds, sew a garland of popcorn, grain cereals, and dried fruits to hang in trees. Or smear peanut butter on pine cones and sprinkle with seeds. Remember to place these where greedy squirrels might not be able to get to them.

Squirrels, however, are very clever and can hang upside down to feed. One idea is to leave an ear of corn out for the squirrels so they won't bother the birds' food.

Have you ever seen squirrels busily burying nuts in the fall? How do they know where to find them later? Squirrels do remember the general area in which they buried nuts, but they rely on their sense of smell to locate buried nuts. Count out 20 unshelled peanuts. Have your child put them in secret hiding places around the house. You may want to keep a list of the places. Wait two days. Then have your child search for the nuts. How many nuts did he or she find? How did your child find them?

Math

Take math into the kitchen where you and your child can make animal-theme foods for a snack or meal. Here are two suggestions.

Hippo-Hip Hooray Salad
For each salad: one lettuce leaf, one pear half, cheese triangles, 2 raisins, 2 cherries

1. Place a lettuce leaf on a plate.
2. Top with a pear half, placing the sliced side down.
3. Add cheese triangle ears, raisin eyes and cherry nose.
   Make one salad for each family member.

A Hoot of a Treat
For each treat: one slice of wheat bread, tuna or chicken salad,
2 slices of egg and black olives, 1 triangle of cheese, pine nuts

1. Cut the bread on one end to form owl's head.
2. Cover the bread with a favorite spread.
3. Place 2 egg slices with black olive slices for eyes.
4. Add a cheese beak and pine nuts for claws. Enjoy!

Answers

Pages 2–3
Bank, Firehouse, Grocery, Hospital, Post Office, School, Toy Shop, Zippity Zoo

Page 7

Page 11
1. snake   2. swan
3. spider   4. skunk
5. slug   6. starfish

```
x  b  s  k  u  n  k
v  s  t  o  p  s  g
s  w  a  n  g  n  s
f  t  r  y  c  o  l
t  u  f  z  j  w  u
s  p  i  d  e  r  g
y  o  s  n  a  k  e
p  q  h  s  n  a  p
```

Page 14
Circle Jan, Bob, Chan, and Lisa.
1. Bob   2. Jan   3. Lisa   4. Chan

Pages 4–5

4. Answers will vary.
5. yes
6. yes
7. no

Page 8
fast, stop, top, pat, ten, tent, tub, bat at, trap, rap, pot; *counterclockwise*: fat, top, par, part, tab, but, net, tap, pot, pots

Page 12
missing numerals: 4, 3, 6, 5, 6, 9, 6, 10, 8, 11, 6

Page 15
1. Jungle World
2. Quackers Pond
3. Zebra Park
4. Monkey Island
Bear Cave

Page 19
1. slide
2. jump
3. dig
4. climb

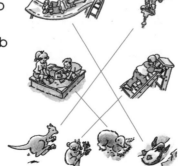

Page 6
1. swan   2. bobcat   3. zebra

Page 9
number words: five, one, four, four, one, three, three, one, two, two, one, one, one
words that rhyme with tip: 1. dip
2. slip 3. trip 4. flip; other words: chip, clip, drip, hip, grip, lip, nip, rip, ship, sip, skip, snip, yip, zip

Page 10
1. 3	2. 6
3. 3 or 8	4. 2
5. 4	6. 1

Page 13
1. under   2. on   3. over
4. across   5. in

page 16
$4 + 3 = 7$ tigers
$6 + 3 = 9$ leopards
$4 + 2 = 6$ bobcats
$5 + 4 = 9$ lions

Pages 17–18
1. Names will vary.	2. $1 + 2 = 3$
3. $3 - 1 = 2$	4. $2 + 3 = 5$
5. $5 - 2 = 3$	6. $3 + 3 = 6$
7. $6 - 2 = 4$	8. $4 - 4 = 0$

Page 20

1. pup   2. cub

Pages 21–22
1. robin
2. fish
3. snake
4. chick

Page 25
1. $6 + 4 = 10$ 2. $5 - 4 = 1$
3. $4 + 2 = 6$ 4. $5 - 3 = 2$
5. $7 + 5 = 12$ 6. $5 - 2 = 3$

Page 26
1. wet   2. huge
3. tiny   4. sleepy
5. long   6. tall

Page 30

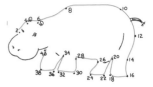

	1	2	3	4	5	6	7	8	9	10
tiger cub										
baby porcupine										
fox										
snowy owl										
fawn										
opossum										
weight in pounds	1	2	3	4	5	6	7	8	9	10

Pages 32–33

mountain; tiger; 12; river or stream; porcupine; 5; palm tree;
zebra; box or fox; 8; rainbow; anteater; bear or bare;
pond; 9; 1; trees or forest; panda; 6; snake; tulip
or flower; penguin; block or black; waterfall; sheep

Page 23

1. can't   Where is
2. Let's   can not
3. Where's   is not
4. isn't   Let us

Page 27
1. 14
2. 2

Page 31

Put In	Take Out	How Many Are Left?	Put In	Put In	How Many in All?
9	2	7	9	6	15
10	4	6	2	8	10
12	7	5	6	5	11
8	6	2	7	7	14
15	8	7	8	6	14

Page 24
1. Tuesday   2. Thursday
3. Monday   4. Saturday

Page 28
glad: happy, sad
noisy: loud, quiet
little: small, big
quick: fast, slow

Page 29
Animal names will vary.
Stories will vary. Make sure that
stories have two characters that
solve a problem.

Page 34
1. Ben
2. Anna
3. Mom
4. Dad

Page 35

1. fat
2. water
3. grass
4. hippo

Page 36
1. to the water fountain
2. flag
3. parrot
4. 2, 1, 3

5.

Page 37

5	10	6	22	13	8
11	15	7	18	31	14
17	20	25	32	47	71
36	22	30	35	40	48
51	56	43	33	45	50

Page 38

1.
2.
3.

4.

Page 39

Drawings will vary.

Page 40

Page 41

1. o p o s s u m
2. d e e r
3. s k u n k
4. s q u i r r e l

Riddles will vary.

Page 42

6:00   9:30   7:00

5:30   8:00   7:30

Page 43

1. B
2. E
3. A
4. D
5. C

Page 44

Kinds of Animals		Animals We Want	Animals We Have	How Many More Do We Need?
camel		8	4	4
deer		15	9	6
giraffe		10	7	3
hippo		12	8	4
pig		14	7	7
sheep		18	9	9
buffalo		9	5	4
moose		13	6	7

Page 45

5 +8	12 −6	8 +2	5 +7	10 −3
13 −7	6 +3	10 −5	12 −6	7 +7
6 +4	9 +3	5 +7	6 +8	14 −6
10	12	12	14	8

moose

Page 46

Page 47

1. No
2. No
3. Yes
4. tracks
5. the forest
6. last night

Page 48

2. 25¢ 25¢ 25¢ 10¢ 1¢; Yes
3. 25¢ 10¢ 10¢ 10¢ 10¢; Yes
4. 25¢ 10¢ 10¢ 5¢ 5¢; No

Page 49

1. 20¢
    +75¢
    ————
    95¢

2. 44¢
    +50¢
    ————
    94¢

3. 42¢
    +34¢
    ————
    76¢

4. 35¢
    +52¢
    ————
    87¢

Page 50

$\frac{1}{2}$ $\frac{1}{4}$

$\frac{1}{3}$ $\frac{2}{2}$

$\frac{3}{4}$ $\frac{2}{3}$

Page 51

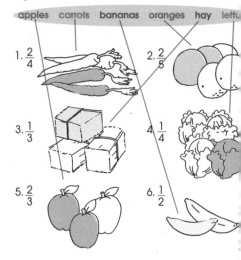

1. $\frac{2}{4}$ 2. $\frac{2}{5}$

3. $\frac{1}{3}$ 4. $\frac{1}{4}$

5. $\frac{2}{3}$ 6. $\frac{1}{2}$

Page 52

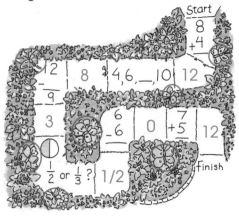

8 butterflies

Page 53

Letters will vary but should follow correct letter form.

Pages 54–55

1. long tails
2. short tails
3. Bears' tails changed because Bear froze his tail in the pond and broke it off when he pulled it out of the ice.

Page 56

Guesses will vary. ☐

Page 57

Reasons children like zoos will vary.